12/14

Lexile: _____

AR/BL: _____

AR Points: _____

YOUR LAND
AND
MY LAND
ASIA

We Visit

MALAYSIA

John

Bankston

Mitchell Lane

PUBLISHERS
P.O. Box 196
Hockessin, Delaware 19707

YOUR LAND AND MY LAND
ASIA

Cambodia
China
India
Indonesia
Japan
Malaysia
North Korea
The Philippines
Singapore
South Korea

YOUR LAND AND MY LAND ASIA

We Visit

MALAYSIA

PUBLISHERS

Printing   1   2   3   4   5   6   7   8   9

Asia

Library of Congress Cataloging-in-Publication Data
Bankston, John, 1974–
  We visit Malaysia / by John Bankston.
      pages cm. — (Your land and my land: Asia)
  Includes bibliographical references and index.
  ISBN 978-1-61228-482-8 (library bound)
  1. Malaysia—Juvenile literature. I. Title.
  DS592.B18 2013
  959.5—dc23
                                              2013033974
eBook ISBN: 9781612285375

PBP

Contents

Introduction

The continent of Asia is the largest on earth, covering almost one-third of the total land area and encompassing nearly 50 different countries. It also has the most people—60 percent of the world's population lives in Asia. Every major religion in the world today got its start in Asia, including Islam, Judaism, Buddhism, Hinduism, and Christianity.

One of the regions of Asia is Southeast Asia. It includes the countries of Myanmar (formerly known as Burma), Thailand, Laos, Vietnam, Cambodia, Indonesia, Singapore, Brunei, the Philippines, East Timor, and Malaysia. Consisting of 13 states and three federal territories, modern Malaysia is a country in two parts. One part, East Malaysia, is on the northern coast of Borneo. Here the states of Sabah and Sarawak share the island with two other countries—Indonesia and Brunei. The other part lies on the Malay Peninsula.

Part of Southeast Asia crosses the equator. Malaysia is just ten miles (16 kilometers) north of this geographic line. Like all countries near the equator, Malaysia is very hot and rarely cooler than 50° F (10° C). The country is usually quite humid as well, with a rainy season stretching from November to February. It gets between 100 to 200 inches (254 to 508 centimeters) of rain a year.

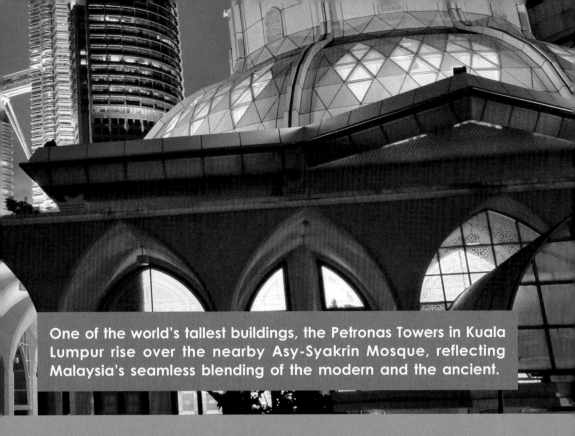

One of the world's tallest buildings, the Petronas Towers in Kuala Lumpur rise over the nearby Asy-Syakrin Mosque, reflecting Malaysia's seamless blending of the modern and the ancient.

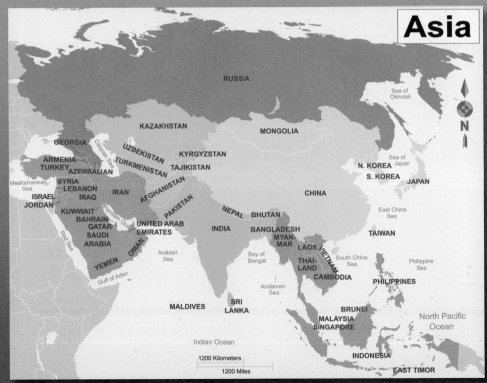

Asia

RUSSIA

Sea of Okhotsk

KAZAKHSTAN

MONGOLIA

GEORGIA

Caspian Sea

UZBEKISTAN

KYRGYZSTAN

Sea of Japan

ARMENIA

TURKEY

AZERBAIJAN

TURKMENISTAN

TAJIKISTAN

N. KOREA

S. KOREA

JAPAN

Mediterranean Sea

SYRIA

LEBANON

IRAN

AFGHANISTAN

CHINA

ISRAEL

JORDAN

IRAQ

Persian Gulf

PAKISTAN

NEPAL

BHUTAN

East China Sea

KUWWAIT

BAHRAIN

QATAR

SAUDI ARABIA

UNITED ARAB EMIRATES

INDIA

BANGLADESH

MYAN-MAR

TAIWAN

Red Sea

OMAN

Arabian Sea

Bay of Bengal

LAOS

VIETNAM

THAI-LAND

South China Sea

Philippine Sea

YEMEN

Gulf of Aden

CAMBODIA

PHILIPPINES

Andaman Sea

MALDIVES

SRI LANKA

BRUNEI

MALAYSIA

SINGAPORE

North Pacific Ocean

Indian Ocean

1200 Kilometers

1200 Miles

INDONESIA

EAST TIMOR

N

Farms like this tea plantation benefit from Malaysia's ample rainfall and lengthy growing season.

Welcome to Malaysia! You might be surprised to know that most of Malaysia was once almost entirely covered by rainforests. Although logging and farming have reduced the size of the rainforest, today nearly two-thirds of the country still boasts some of the world's oldest tropical evergreen forests. Even in Kuala Lumpur, the country's capital and largest city, pristine parkland is close by its tallest buildings.

More than 100 miles (160 kilometers) away, the Cameron Highlands offers a break from Malaysia's tropical heat. At over 3,500 feet (1,070 meters) above sea level, its temperatures rarely climb above 70°F (21°C). The area is an agricultural center with numerous tea gardens.

Natural landscapes are often accessible to visitors. One trek is along the Central or Buffalo Range. These heavily forested mountains cross the center of the country for 300 miles (480 kilometers) before entering Thailand. Across the South China Sea, the state of Sabah is the site of Mount Kinabalu. The tallest peak in Southeast Asia at 13,435 feet (4,095 meters), it can be scaled without special training or equipment by people who are in good physical condition.

Separated by the Buffalo Mountain Range, Malaysia's coasts had limited contact with each other before the 20th century. Malaysia's west coast grew rapidly as it attracted explorers and traders. The east coast of the Malay Peninsula, along with Sarawak and Sabah, are far less developed. Many communities there are especially conservative. Muslim women often wear head coverings while men dress in skullcaps. Tourists visiting cities might wear shorts and tank tops but are advised

Named for King George III, Georgetown on Penang Island features century-old British architecture and traditional Chinese shophouses.

to dress more modestly in places like Kota Bharu. The northernmost city in Malaysia, Kota Bharu lies on the east coast of Peninsular Malaysia. Deeply Muslim, the city is well-known for friendly locals, a popular night market, and traditional shadow puppets.

Across the country, the west coast island of Penang is home to Georgetown. Named after British King George III, the city is a good place to see Southeast Asia as it once was. The country's British colonial past is evident here, as is the impact of Chinese immigration. Many buildings were constructed over 100 years ago. Some reflect Britain's influence, while ramshackle shophouses in the Chinese quarter line the street and heavenly lanterns overhead cast a reddish glow.

FYI FACT:

Called wayang kulit, shadow puppetry in Malaysia tells mythical stories of right and wrong. The puppets are usually made from leather and are moved using sticks made from buffalo horns. An oil or halogen lamp projects light through a piece of cloth. When the puppets are placed before it they cast shadows against a wall or screen.

Longhouses like this one in Sarawak house dozens of families who work together growing crops like pepper and rubber.

Most Malaysians once lived and worked on small farms, but today Malaysia is increasingly becoming an urban country. More than half of its people live in cities like Kuala Lumpur and Georgetown, which attract young people who want better job opportunities and a wider variety of fun activities.

The rural areas of Malaysia are still home to rubber plantations and tin mines. These can be difficult and dangerous places to work. The most rural part of the country lies in the state of Sarawak, where longhouses stretch for several hundred feet and hold dozens of families. The contrast between old and new can be seen in the satellite dishes dotting traditional longhouse roofs.

Built from hardwood and bamboo, the longhouses sit atop stilts with livestock underneath. Open verandahs are used for drying rice, pepper, and rubber. On the opposite end, the community often gathers inside the closed verandahs. Between them are apartments for families.

Travelers can easily arrange to visit a longhouse. There they can meet the tribal chief and visit the community's pepper and fruit orchards or rubber plantations. A special time to visit is during the Gawai Dayak harvest festival celebrations in late May and early June. During this event, many young people who left for Malaysia's cities return to the longhouses where they grew up.

The wildlife refuges of Sarawak and Sabah reveal Malaysia as it looked millions of years ago, when Southeast Asian islands were linked in a large land mass covered by tropical rainforests. Today naturalists call the islands and the waters which separate them "Sundaland."

For many, the best part of visiting exotic locales is seeing unusual animals. Explorer Marco Polo described one as a man with a tail who lived in the mountains. Today we know it by its Malay name: orangutan. With their deep-set eyes, grasping hands, and scruffy orange "beards," it's easy to see their resemblance to tiny, wizened old people.

Logging has reduced the habitat of these forest dwellers and they are considered endangered. They can best be seen at the Sepilok Orang Utan Rehabilitation Center in Sandakan on the east coast of Sabah. The largest orangutan sanctuary in the world, it cares for hundreds of orphans before releasing them into the wild.

Orangutans are famous for their long arms which when outstretched can measure seven feet (2.1 meters) from fingertip to fingertip. Because of this and a fearsome call that can be heard from a mile away, they are often mistaken for aggressive predators. Instead, they keep to themselves, eating fruit and leaves.

One of Malaysia's most fascinating hunters is not an animal at all. It's a plant. This round or tube-shaped growth lies on the ground or hangs like a leaf. The largest carnivorous plant on earth, the pitcher

The meat-eating pitcher plant is deadly to insects and small animals.

plant consumes whatever is small and unlucky enough to get trapped inside by the fluid inside its bottom. Its prey ranges from insects to larger creatures like rats and even small birds.

West Malaysia's protected forests offer their own trip back in time. Along the southeastern peninsula, the land inside Endau Rompin National Park has changed little in more than 260 million years. One of West Malaysia's few remaining lowland forests, it is best visited with a tour guide. Besides helping to erect a campsite, guides often take visitors to the Sungai Selai River and one of its breathtaking waterfalls.

Lucky visitors get to see the Sumatran rhinoceros. The smallest member of the rhinoceros family, these 1,700-pound (770 kilograms) beasts can reach a length of 10 feet (3 meters) and stand almost five feet tall (1.5 meters) at the shoulders. Less than 400 exist in the wild. They also rarely breed in zoos. When one was born at the Cincinnati Zoo in 2001, it was the first one born in captivity in nearly 100 years.

Malaysia is home to the Malayan sun bear. These tree-dwelling creatures are just half the size of the American black bear. Weighing only 150 pounds (68 kg), they get their name from the bib-like patch of golden or white fur decorating their necks. Despite their name, the bears rarely see the sun as they prefer to sleep during the day.

Malaysia is also home to clouded leopards, tigers, a variety of monkeys, and numerous other animals. One of the best places to observe them is at Taman Negara (which means "national park" in Malay), a half-day trek from Kuala Lumpur. Encompassing 1,677 square miles (4,434 square kilometers) of jungle, it was founded in 1937 and is the oldest national park in the country. It attracts over 60,000 visitors every year hoping to see the park's 100 tigers and over 600 elephants (the largest population in Southeast Asia).

The park is also home to Malaysia's oldest culture, the Batek or Orang Asli ("original people" in Malay). Several hundred of them live inside the boundaries of Taman Negara, existing as they have for thousands of years. Still, the best evidence of Malaysia's earliest people lies not in the jungle, but within caves with paintings created over 40,000 years ago.

Where in the World

Rising over 13,000 feet (4,000 meters), Sabah's Mount Kinabalu, along with the nearby St. John and South Peaks, are popular attractions for mountain climbers.

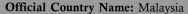

MALAYSIA FACTS AT A GLANCE

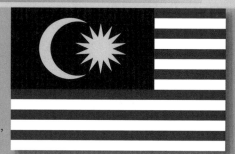

Official Country Name: Malaysia

Official Language: Bahasa Malaysia; English, Chinese, Tamil, Telugu, Malayalam, Panjabi, and Thai are also spoken

Population: 29,179,952 (July 2012 estimate)

Land Area: 127,216 square miles (329,847 square kilometers), slightly larger than New Mexico

Capital: Kuala Lumpur

Government: constitutional monarchy

Ethnic Makeup: Malay 50.4%, Chinese 23.7%, indigenous 11%, Indian 7.1%, others 7.8% (2004 est.)

Religions: Islam 60.4%, Buddhist 19.2%, Christian 9.1%, Hindu 6.3%, Confucianism, Taoism, other traditional Chinese religions 2.6%, other or unknown 1.5%, none 0.8% (2000 census)

Exports: electronic equipment, petroleum and liquefied natural gas, wood and wood products, palm oil, rubber, textiles, chemicals

Imports: electronics, machinery, petroleum products, plastics, vehicles, iron and steel products, chemicals

Crops: Peninsular Malaysia—palm oil, rubber, cocoa, rice; Sabah—palm oil, subsistence crops, rubber, timber; Sarawak—palm oil, rubber, timber, pepper

Average Temperatures: 90.5°F (32.5°C)

Average Annual Rainfall: 100 inches (254 cm)

Highest Point: Mount Kinabalu - 13,435 feet (4,095 meters)

Lowest Point: South China Sea – sea level

Longest River: Rajang River, Sarawak - 350 miles (563 kilometers)

National Flag: Based on the design of the U.S. flag, the Malaysian flag is often referred to as Jalur Gemilang ("Stripes of Glory"). It has 14 equal horizontal stripes of red alternating with white, which stand for the equal status in the federation of the 13 member states and the federal government. A blue rectangle in the upper hoist-side corner bears a yellow crescent and a yellow 14-pointed star. The 14 points on the star represent the unity between the states and the government. The crescent is a traditional symbol of Islam. Blue symbolizes the unity of the Malay people and yellow is the royal color of Malay rulers.

National Sports: sepak takraw (kick volleyball) and badminton

National Anthem: "Negaraku" ("My Country")

Sources: CIA World Factbook: Malaysia - https://www.cia.gov/library/publications/the-world-factbook/geos/my.html

USA Today Travel Tips - http://traveltips.usatoday.com/rivers-malaysia-63251.html

World Weather Online - http://www.worldweatheronline.com/Kuala-Lumpur-weather/Kuala-Lumpur/MY.aspx?cup=1304101513

Malacca's well-located harbor attracted the interest of several European countries. These countries were seeking a sea route to compete with Italian traders who controlled many of the land routes to Asia.

Malaysian History

East Malaysia's Niah Cave was no secret. Nineteenth-century naturalist Alfred Russel Wallace wrote about an enormous cave 10 miles inland from the South China Sea. The largest of its five openings was 300 feet high (91 meters) by 600 feet (182 meters) across. Yet much of the cave's interior remained unexplored until it was purchased by the Sarawak Museum. It was the job of curator Tom Harrison to decide what to exhibit and where to explore. In 1954, he led the first formal expedition of the Niah Cave.

Deep inside the cave, Harrison and his team reached a well-lit, dry area which would soon be known as "the painted cave." The cave's walls were stained by a reddish rock called hematite. Ancient paintings decorated its ceiling. This was the first clue that people once lived there.

Amidst the rubble covering the cave floor, Harrison's team found human bones. They had been well-preserved by the hot, dry conditions. Testing revealed that an intact skeleton was a teenage boy who'd died over 40,000 years ago.

There is no recorded history of Malaysia's first people. What we know of them comes from observers who wrote about early Malaysians and remnants like cooking pots and bones.

Malaysia's population grew from several major waves of immigration. The first came from Tibet and China, traveling south through Thailand to Malaysia. Others island-hopped and made short journeys over water.

FYI FACT:

The oldest museum in Borneo, the Sarawak Museum was built in 1891. It specializes in local arts and culture. Thanks to a sympathetic Japanese officer, it survived World War II intact.

The first settlers, the Orang Asli, reached Malaysia around 3000 BCE. These "original people" lived in the forest and survived by hunting and gathering, living on what they could kill or find. It was a difficult and unreliable way to live. Today some 150,000 of them remain in Malaysia. Many survive in the rainforest as they have for thousands of years.

While the Orang Asli settled in the forest, another group of early arrivals settled near the coastline. The Orang Laut, or "sea people," were nomadic, traveling from place to place. They survived by fishing and piracy. Today thousands still remain.

Two thousand years later, a group of people who spoke what became the Malay language also settled in Southeast Asia. They mainly lived in Sumatra and West Malaysia. Many were farmers and skilled sailors who had traveled from Taiwan, an island east of China.

Scientists who study people and how they once lived are called anthropologists. Modern anthropologists disagree with older theories suggesting that when the new people reached what is now Malaysia in 1000 BCE, they killed or enslaved the native hunter-gathers. Instead, the current belief is that the Malays probably lived alongside them. Eventually the two groups intermarried while the natives gained fishing and farming skills.

By 500 BCE, Malay sailors understood how to use the monsoon winds which arrived from the south in late May and from the north in November. They could also use the ocean's swell and wave patterns, cloud formations, and even the flight paths of birds to set the proper course. Some reached the coast of Africa.

Traders from China and India began arriving in Malaysia around 100 BCE. Indians introduced Hindu and Buddhist beliefs which were adopted by the Malays. These religions blended with an ancient belief called animism. Believers see the world as guided by spirits living in mountains and caves, on the tops of trees, and in the rivers. Angry

An Orang Asli couple in their hut in the Cameron Highlands. There are 18 Orang Asli tribes. More than three-fourths of them live in poverty.

spirits are responsible for failed crops and droughts. To make the spirits happy, believers sacrificed animals and occasionally the unlucky captive.

Knowledge of the region's attractions quickly spread. As guidebook author Simon Richmond points out, "By the 2nd century CE Malaya was known as far away as Europe. Ptolemy, the Greek geographer, labeled it 'Aurea Chersonesus' (Golden Chersonese); it was believed the area was rich in gold."[1]

Merchant ships navigating the Strait of Malacca entered the Indian Ocean or traveled to Middle Eastern ports. South of Malaysia, the region was dominated by the Majapahit Empire, which ruled from Java (part of modern-day Indonesia).

Around 1390, a Sumatran prince named Parameswara attacked a port south of Malaysia. After taking it over, he renamed it Singapore. Soon after a rival army defeated him, Parameswar left in search of a new home. He didn't have to go far. Traveling along the west coast of the Malay Peninsula, Parameswara was hunting one day. Stopping for a rest beneath a tree, he watched his dogs pursuing a mouse deer, a small animal native to the region. Without warning, the creature turned and chased the dogs. They were so startled that they dove into the ocean.

Parameswara believed it was a sign. He decided to build a trading port there, and named it after the malacca tree where he had been resting.

Located along the Strait of Malacca, the new port attracted Chinese, Arab, and Indian traders. Since it collected a fee every time goods were bought or sold, it soon became very rich. Some traders brought more than gold, spices or silks: a new religion, one which continues to influence Malaysia more than 500 years later.

The Crystal Mosque in Terengganu was built in 2008 on the island of Wan Man in the state of Terengganu. The primary building materials were steel, glass, and crystal. It serves as the centerpiece of the Islamic Heritage Park.

Chapter 3

Growth of Empires

According to Islam, in 610 an Arab named Muhammad was visited by the angel Gabriel near the city of Mecca on the Arabian Peninsula. For the rest of Muhammad's life, Gabriel gave him verses from God. These became the Qur'an, Islam's holy book. To believers, Muhammad was the last in a line of prophets who included Abraham and Jesus.

Islam arrived in Malaysia via either Indian or Arab traders in the 12th century. After Hindu ruler Phra Ong Mahawangsa converted to Islam, he became the peninsula's first sultan, or Muslim ruler. The faith grew after Parameswara's son, Mahkota Iskander Shah, converted to Islam following his father's death in 1414. By then large numbers of people throughout Malaysia, Indonesia, and Borneo were converting. Shah inherited a growing empire.

The area's fortunes had improved even more a few years earlier, after Chinese admiral Zheng He promised to protect Parameswara from Thai attacks. After the agreement, large numbers of Chinese men moved there. Many married Malay women.

Presiding over his sultanate, Mahkota Iskander Shah encouraged the spread of Islam. Because the empire's leaders were Muslim, traders and merchants figured they would have a better chance of being successful if they converted. By the end of the 1400s, the sultan ruled over where Malaysia is today along with Singapore and Sumatra's east coast. Over 100,000 people lived in Malacca and the port held hundreds of ships at a time. Its success did not go unnoticed.

This drawing of Malacca by artist Francis Valentijn dates back to about 1726, when it was under Dutch control. Dutch merchant ships and smaller local craft dot the harbor. St. Paul's Church is on the hill on the left side, while the A Famosa fortress is beneath the church.

One thousand years ago, the inventions, silks, and spices of mainland Asia were carried overland to Italy. Italian merchants sold the goods across Europe. Seeking a water route to end Italian trade dominance, European countries like the Netherlands, Spain, and especially Portugal soon discovered the ports of Southeast Asia. The one founded by Parameswar seemed ideal.

FYI FACT:

During the fall, Malaysian Muslims celebrate Hari Ray Haji. This is when many Muslims make the required once-in-a-lifetime journey to Muhammad's birthplace of Mecca.

Malaysia prides itself on religious freedom. As the country's second-largest religious group, Buddhists have constructed numerous temples and statues like this one honoring the religion's founder, Buddha.

Celebrate!

For an entire month, Muslims fast from sunrise to sunset. They don't eat or drink. They continue going to work or to school while also praying, reading the Qur'an, and doing good works. This is Ramadan, one of the five pillars of Islam.

Because 60 percent of Malaysians are Muslims, Ramadan affects the rhythm of life across the country. The celebration marking its conclusion is impossible to ignore. The Festival of Fast Breaking, known as either *Eid Al-Fitr* or Hari Lebanon, is one of the country's many public holidays. It is celebrated with family gatherings and presents. Because so many city dwellers visit relatives along the rural, traditionally Muslim east coast, it can be difficult for tourists to find hotel rooms at that time.

Malaysian Muslims grow up accustomed to the religion's rituals. They only eat halal food, which is prepared according to Islamic law. Rising at dawn, the city's Muslims face Mecca and offer their morning prayers. They heed four more calls for prayer throughout the day, in honor of Salah, another pillar of Islam.

The Malaysian government honors the faith's religious holidays, closing offices and public roads during parades. Malaysia's constitution protects other beliefs, noting that "Islam is the religion of the Federation; but other religions may be practiced in peace and harmony in any part of the Federation."[1]

Public holidays are not exclusively based on Islam. Malaysia is in the top 10 for most days off among all the countries in the world. This

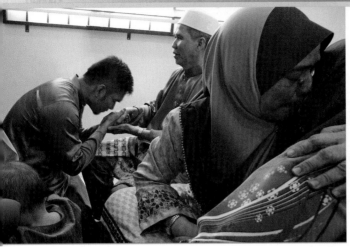

Ramadan requires the Muslim faithful to fast from dawn to dusk throughout its month-long duration. At its conclusion, Muslims celebrate Eid with an exchange of food, gifts, wishes, and blessings.

is because Malaysia also honors its large populations of Buddhists, Christians, and Hindus. These religions all enjoy celebrations.

Malaysian Buddhists follow the religion's core belief that happiness can only be achieved by eliminating desire. Their most important holiday is the birthday of Buddha, the religion's founder. Falling on the first full moon in May, Vesak Day is celebrated by chanting prayers at temples, performing acts of kindness, and releasing caged birds.

The New Year doesn't begin on January 1st for Malaysia's Chinese population. Their New Year celebrations mark the beginning of the Lunar New Year, which arrives between late January and early February. Decorations include lanterns, cherry blossoms, and orange trees while the color red is everywhere. Most Malaysian states have a two-day holiday, allowing Chinese residents to visit with family members. Usually these gatherings feature large meals of chicken, pork, and fish with the first course being yee sang—raw fish salad. According

FYI FACT:

Hindus, Muslims, and Chinese follow a lunar calendar. Each month begins with the new moon. It only takes 354 days for the moon to pass through its phases twelve times. Therefore, the lunar year is shorter than the 365-day year observed in most countries. A shorter, intercalary month may be added periodically to bring the two calendars together.

With its large Chinese population, Malaysia is awash in lanterns and fireworks during the run-up to the Lunar New Year. Here the Rek Lok Si is lighted in Pulau Pinang, the island on which Georgetown is located.

to tradition, the higher the salad is tossed, the more the tosser's fortunes will grow. Across the country, streets are closed for dragon dancers and pedestrian parades. Children and unmarried adults receive red envelopes stuffed with money while Chinese businesses forgive debtors.

Two Chinese celebrations in the late summer and early fall honor unique spirits. During the Festival of the Seven Sisters, unmarried Chinese girls pray to the weaving maid for good husbands. Later, the invisible guests at the Festival of the Hungry Ghosts eat only the "spirits" of the holiday's delicious feasts. Afterward, the faithful enjoy the food.

Malaysia's Hindu population has its share of holidays. In January, Thai Pongal celebrates the month of "Thai." The luckiest of all the months, it is celebrated with food offerings such as sugar, rice, and milk.

Later in the month, the Thaipusam Festival honors Murugan, the Hindu god of war and victory. At the Batu Caves outside of Kuala

At the Batu Caves, the Golden Statue of Lord Murugan looms over participants during the Thaipusam Festival. The festival is one of the most-recorded Hindi rites, with tape of the event broadcast worldwide.

Lumpur, a huge gold statue waits at the foot of the Temple Cave. One million celebrants gather outside while a few faithful climb the temple's 272 steps to the cave. Their efforts are challenged by complex steel arches called Kavadi piercing their skin. Others pierce their tongues, lips and cheeks with hooks and hang fruit from the metal.

Most participants survive none the worse for wear. There are even treatments with lemon and ash to keep the injuries from scarring. Despite these precautions, doctors are kept busy treating those who overdo it.

Deepavali, or Diwali, is a less-painful Hindu public holiday. Sometimes known as the festival of lights, it honors Lord Rama's victory over the demon king Ravana. It also celebrates the victory of good over evil and each person's inner light. Because it is believed that Lakshmi, the god of wealth, won't enter an unlit home, Hindu houses are brightly lit. Families start the day with an oil bath and enjoy the holiday with new clothes and lots of sweets.

The Festival of Light, or Deepavali, takes place in late fall as Malaysia's nearly two million Hindi celebrate the victory of good over evil, of light over darkness.

Many Hindu families have an open house during the holiday, inviting people of other races and religions into their home. As the *Times of India* explains, "What the festival of lights really stands for today is a reaffirmation of hope, a renewed commitment to friendship and goodwill and a religiously sanctioned celebration of the simple—and some not so simple—joys of life."[2]

For Christians, the biggest and most important celebration is Christmas. In Malaysia it is a public holiday. As in many countries, shopping centers are decorated and Christians welcome visiting family members with gifts and food.

Nearly 10 percent of the country is Christian, with the majority in Sarawak and Sabah. The faith arrived in Malaysia in the seventh century. Most natives were not exposed to the religion until the early 1500s when Europeans began landing on the Malay Peninsula's shores. The new arrivals were interested in converts. Those who didn't convert could be killed.

Explorations by men like Portugal's Vasco da Gama brought Europeans to Malaysian shores as they sought both trade opportunities and Christian converts.

Chapter 5

Europeans Arrive

Spices such as cinnamon and nutmeg sprinkled on oatmeal, along with the pepper that added a "kick" to eggs, came from islands such as Borneo, Sumatra, and Java. Shipped from the sultanate of Malacca to eager buyers half a world away via a long overland route called the Silk Road, the spice trade made many people in the empire rich.

It did the same thing for a number of Europeans, especially Italians. Other European countries didn't want Italy controlling the spice trade. The solution was to find a sea route.

In the 1400s, Portuguese fishermen and merchants sailed deep into the Atlantic Ocean and then along the west coast of Africa. In 1498 Portuguese explorer Vasco da Gama rounded the Cape of Good Hope in South Africa and eventually came to India. Eleven years later, the Portuguese were the first Europeans to land at Malacca. Crowds gathered to greet them, taking off their hats and twisting their beards. When they returned to their ships, the Malaccans attacked them. A number of Portuguese were killed or captured. The survivors returned home.

The Portuguese refused to back down. In 1511, a flotilla of 18 heavily armed ships sped toward Malacca. Led by Alfonso de Albuquerque, the Portuguese defeated 20,000 men defending the port with war elephants, cannons, and firearms. Numerous Portuguese also died. The deposed sultan fled south, establishing a new empire called Johor-Riau, which would extend to Singapore.

Tome Pires, a Portuguese druggist and diplomat, wrote about the importance of Malacca, explaining that "you find what you want and sometimes more than you are looking for. [There was] no trading port as large as Malacca...nor anywhere they deal in such fine and highly prized merchandise. Goods from all over the East are found here; goods from all over the West are sold here....Whoever is lord of Malacca has his hand on the throat of Venice [The most important Italian trading city]."[1]

The victors constructed a fort called A Famosa to provide protection. Visitors today can tour the site, pausing by the archway—the only item rescued from demolition over two centuries ago. Besides A Famosa, the Portuguese also built a customs house to collect port fees. But they were interested in more than just money.

Most Europeans shared Pires' feelings when he wrote, "Alfonso de Albuquerque...never ceases fighting against the name of Mohammed... [God] wills to make Christianity take root throughout your kingdoms. [This only happened because of] an immense expenditure of money such as no Christian King has ever made before."[2]

The Portuguese built St Paul's church in 1521 and brought in priests led by St. Francis Xavier. They planned to convert the locals to Christianity. They were soon in over their heads.

FYI FACT:

Many buildings in Malacca dating from the 1500s are in very poor condition. St. Paul's Church has been in ruins over 150 years. For history buffs, the best bets are the numerous museums in Malacca's town center: the Architecture Museum, the Maritime Museum, and the Islam Museum. Besides St. Paul's, the oldest Christian church in Malaysia, Malacca also boasts the country's oldest active mosque and oldest Buddhist temple.

Malacca was under constant attack. The sultan of Johor-Riau never abandoned his dream of taking it back. Other Muslim-ruled states viewed the Portuguese as Christian invaders. They regularly assaulted the port. Most Muslim, Chinese, Arab, and Indian merchants avoided trading with the new arrivals. On the water, rival Malay states encouraged pirate attacks against ships traveling through the Strait of Malacca.

Now in ruins, the A Famosa fortress once guarded Malacca's port.

As Malacca's trade declined, the Netherlands' Dutch East India Company grew stronger. They gained territory in Indonesia and controlled ports along western Java. In 1640, the Sultan of Johor-Riau joined the Dutch and attacked Malacca. The siege lasted eight months and the Dutch finally overcame the Portuguese defenses early the following year. Despite the hard-fought victory, Malacca's decline continued. The Dutch were focused on Indonesia. While Malacca had been a base for Portuguese interests, the Dutch were headquartered in Jakarta, on the island of Java.

Events in Europe also shifted the balance of power. Britain wanted a trade route to Southeast Asia. In 1786, Francis Light from the British East India Company made a deal with the Sultan of Kedah. The company was allowed to establish itself on Penang.

The English gained more territory soon after Light made his deal. When French leader Napoleon Bonaparte invaded the Netherlands, Britain took over Malacca to keep it from France's control. Although the British handed Malacca back to the Dutch in 1818, by then they had destroyed A Famosa. Malacca faded, but a new city rose to power.

The Twin Towers were built by Petronas, which is short for Petroliam Nasional Berhad, a Malaysian oil and gas company founded in 1974. In 2009, French climber Alain "Spiderman" Robert ascended one of the towers, using only his hands and feet.

Rise of Cities,
Rise of Malaysia

Located midway between Singapore and Thailand, Malaysia's capital city of Kuala Lumpur blends the ancient and the modern. Founded in 1857 by 87 Chinese tin miners, it was named for the spot where the Gombak and Klang Rivers meet. Kuala Lumpur means "muddy river junction." It was an ugly name. It was an ugly time.

The city's founders worked alongside thousands of other Chinese immigrants laboring in the mines. Growing numbers of Malay natives were employed on local farms, producing crops to feed the new arrivals. The work was difficult, even dangerous. Besides the risks of farming and mining, everyone in the country battled swarms of mosquitoes. Many carried malaria—a deadly disease that killed most of Kuala Lumpur's founders.

Yet the city became a place of hope. Today the ambitions of Malaysians are symbolized by the gigantic Petronas Twin Towers. Rising some 1,483 feet (452 meters), the 88-story building was the world's tallest from 1998 to 2004. Part of the "Golden Triangle" of the city, the towers are slimmer than most skyscrapers. The Skyscraper Museum describes its design as answering "the developer's call to express the 'culture and heritage of Malaysia' by evoking Islamic arabesques and employing repetitive geometries characteristic of Muslim architecture...an 8-point star formed by intersecting squares is an obvious reference to Islamic design; curved and pointed bays create a scalloped facade that suggests temple towers. The identical towers

Malaysia's diverse population is reflected in ethnic neighborhoods like this Little India in Kuala Lumpur.

are linked by a bridge at the 41st floor, creating a dramatic gateway to the city."[1]

Besides offering a panoramic view, the towers are encircled by nearly 70 acres of parks and public plazas. Despite crumbling sidewalks, oppressive heat, and a complicated bus system, tourists trying to find their way around the city of a million and a half people are aided by locals well-known for their friendly helpfulness.

Once the property of the Sultan of Selangor, today Kuala Lumpur is home to a national university and branch offices for major corporations. Like towns and cities throughout Malaysia, Islamic mosques, Christian churches, and Chinese temples often coexist within a single neighborhood. So do their congregants. Today many citizens mention having a "Malaysian identity," a sense of being connected despite different backgrounds and cultures.

This does not mean that ethnic communities are rare. Kuala Lumpur, like many cities along the Malay Peninsula, has a Little India. This section of the city offers Muslim and Hindu clothing and flower stalls, along with fresh ingredients for Indian meals. "Banana leaf restaurants" are popular with Indian and non-Indian alike for serving spicy meals wrapped in a banana leaf and eaten by hand.

"Kumpungs" ("villages") still dot the Malay Peninsula. They owe their design to Sir Thomas Stamford Raffles. Raffles began working for the British East India Company (EIC) in 1795, when he was 14 years old. He studied the Malay language and culture while in England, then traveled to the Malay Peninsula. He was a lieutenant governor in Sumatra when he had the idea which altered the peninsula's future.

FYI FACT:

Perhaps the most interesting Chinatown in Malaysia is in Kuala Terengganu. Its traditional shophouses act as upscale boutiques and galleries selling regional art. It also has the oldest Chinese temple in the region.

Sir Thomas Raffles turned his early fascination with Malay culture into a government posting and an opportunity to redesign the region's villages.

Raffles believed Britain should establish a base on its southern tip. By doing that, England could control the Strait of Malacca. His bosses agreed. On February 6, 1819, Raffles signed a treaty which established a trading post on Singapore.

In 1826, Great Britain formed a colony made up of Malacca, Penang, and Singapore called the Straits Settlements. A British corporation took over the northern half of Borneo, which became Sabah. The British placed a representative called a "resident" in each kingdom. The kingdom's sultan had to listen to the resident on politics or economic matters.

The British kept the two main Kuala Lumpur groups, the Malays and the Chinese, separate from each other. This reinforced their ethnic divisions. The British also determined the jobs that each group held. Instead of skills, the workers' race determined what they did for a living!

Tin mines were almost exclusively Chinese. Farms were run by Malays. This division lasted into modern times.

A new group of immigrants arrived with a new industry. In the late 1800s, English botanist Henry Ridley smuggled seeds from Brazilian rubber plants into the region. He spent years trying to convince reluctant Malay farmers, accustomed to growing coffee, to cultivate rubber trees instead. After disease devastated their coffee crops, they finally turned to Ridley's rubber plants.

When the people of Borneo tried to overthrow the sultan, British adventurer James Brook used his riches to end the rebellion. In return, the sultan allowed him to rule part of the island. Brook became raja (or king) of the region where Sarawak is today. He and his descendants ruled for almost a century. The locals called them the "white rajas."

The plants were an immediate success. By the end of the 19th century, bicycles had become popular in many parts of the world. Soon afterward, Ford Motor Company founder Henry Ford designed an assembly line to speed the production of cars and make them less expensive. Millions of bikes and cars used Malay rubber for their tires. To keep up with demand, rubber crops were harvested by a new wave of immigrants—Indians, who were kept separate from the Chinese and Malay populations.

The British maintained control as best they could. In the 1860s and '70s, they put down fights between Chinese tin miners. In the 1900s, they tried to manage conflicts among the three main ethnic groups.

Malaya's success continued with few interruptions until 1929, when the U.S. stock market crashed. The years following the crash are known as the Great Depression. Unemployment grew, as did business and bank failures. Across the world, other countries suffered as well.

Malaya was also affected when Japanese forces invaded the Chinese territory of Manchuria in 1931. Numerous Chinese left the Malay Peninsula to fight alongside their countrymen, while overall immigration into Malaya slowed as factories shut down from the lack of orders due to the Great Depression.

In 1937, Japan launched a full-scale invasion of mainland China. This only deepened the conflict as Western powers like the U.S. and England condemned the invasion. For many people in Japan, however, taking land in China was no different from the colonial conquests by Europeans centuries earlier.

Japanese author Tokutomi Sohō argued that "Japan cannot sit idly by and be resigned to the fate of confinement while being starved to death. It is entirely appropriate for us as a nation to act freely in order to live."[2]

In the early morning hours of December 7, 1941, Japanese forces attacked the U.S. naval base at Pearl Harbor, Hawaii. Japanese troops also landed on southern Thailand and northern Malaya. The invaders

In 1940, workers in a Malayan rubber factory produce sheets of latex, which was then used to produce tires and other products. Growing and processing rubber improved the region's economy, but also increased the numbers of people enduring difficult, dangerous, and low-paying jobs.

perazioni in Malesia: artiglie-
ipponiche autotrainate raggiun-
gono le posizioni (Luce)

**Japanese troops on the move early in 1942. Unlike these men,
most of the invading forces advanced on bicycles or on foot with
a rapidity that astonished British defenders.**

rode bicycles toward the southern end of the Malay Peninsula,
increasing their mobility and overwhelming the British defenders. Well
protected from the water, Singapore was unprepared for the more than
20,000 Japanese soldiers attacking by land. The British surrendered
within a few days. After nearly 150 years of occupation, the defeat
was devastating. Life became very grim. Chinese were singled out—
many were killed or tortured.

It took more than three years and the loss of millions of lives before
the war ended. Despite the horrors of war, Japan had granted the first
official recognition of the Malay language.

With the war over, life in former European colonies such as Malaya
quickly changed.

Tunku Abdul Rahman declares the independence of what was then known as the Federation of Malaya in 1957. He became the new nation's first prime minister. Merdeka Stadium had been built in less than a year to host the ceremony.

Chapter 7

A New Malaysia

Continental Europe had been a battlefield, and much of it lay in ruins. Countries like England shifted their focus to rebuilding themselves, not their empires. On the Malay Peninsula and in colonies across the globe, the war's end cultivated a desire for independence.

Speaking two decades after the war, Singapore's Prime Minister Lee Kuan Yew undoubtedly expressed the feelings of many Malaysians when he said that "My colleagues and I are of that generation that went through the Second World War and the Japanese Occupation and emerged determined that no one—neither the Japanese nor the British—had the right to push and kick us around. We were determined that we could govern ourselves and bring up our children in a country where we can be proud to be self-respecting people."[1]

In 1948, the Malay Peninsula kingdoms, along with Malacca and Penang, became the Federation of Malaya. They remained under British control while Singapore, North Borneo, and Sarawak became separate crown colonies.

As soon as the colonial government in the Federation of Malaya was established, the Malayan Communist Party initiated a rebellion against British rule. British forces responded by moving the rural population into "New Villages." These tightly policed communities made it difficult for the communist insurgency to get food or other support. The rebellion finally ended in 1960.

While it was still was going on, Britain's Sir Gerald Templer organized local councils and elections. Many Malay and Chinese joined with the English to put Malaysia on the path to independence. In 1955, the first elections were held. A political leader named Tunku Abdul Rahman emerged. He would join fellow Malay leaders in the United Malaya National Organization to create a three-party partnership with the Malaysian Chinese Association and the Malayan Indian Congress.

On August 31, 1957, the Federation of Malaya gained complete independence from Great Britain. The country operated under a constitution drawn up with the help of experts from Australia, India, and Pakistan. The new government was a parliamentary democracy, similar to England's. A king would be elected every five years by the nine rulers of the states. In turn, he would appoint the government's cabinet with the prime minister as leader. Two houses of congress, one elected and one appointed, would make the laws.

FYI FACT:

The son of Kedah's sultan, Abdul Rahman (above right) is often called the "Father of Malaysia." Many citizens know him just as "Tunku," which means "my lord." The first prime minister after the country became independent, Rahman is credited with bringing together Malaysia's main ethnic groups.

Rioting and arson nearly destroyed the new nation in 1969 as Malaysia's diverse ethnic groups fought for their rights. Here a soldier stands guard in the Chinese section of Kuala Lumpur.

In 1963, Singapore, Sabah and Sarawak joined Malaya to form a new country called the Federation of Malaysia. Most of Malaysia's Malay majority supported the inclusion of Sabah and Sarawak. They hoped the island's ethnically diverse population would balance out Chinese-led Singapore. Instead, economic and political disputes quickly developed. In 1965, Singapore became independent.

Different ethnic groups still dominated different occupations. The Malays controlled government and agriculture. The Chinese dominated commerce and industry. The Chinese resented the political power of the Malays, while the Malays envied the wealth enjoyed by the Chinese.

In 1969, this anger turned into violence. Bloody riots erupted in Kuala Lumpur. Hundreds of people died in the conflict. The country was tearing itself apart. The government suspended the constitution and upcoming elections. A state of emergency was declared. Many wondered if Malaysia would survive.

Today the Chinatown section of Kuala Lumpur is well known for Petaling Street, one of the best places for shopping in the neighborhood.

20-20 Vision

Malaysia often blends the familiar with the unfamiliar, the traditional with the modern. The sari, a colorful and traditional long Indian garment, is worn by both young and old women, but often the outfit ends in sneakers. Malay and Indian meals served in the country are often eaten by hand (always the right hand), but the diner might also be talking on a cell phone or listening to a personal stereo. Although the country has long blended the old and new, racial and religious harmony is a new development.

In the early 1970s, the country was at a crossroads. Following the deadly riots in the capital and the suspension of elections, Malaysia's leadership set about amending the constitution. Talking about "sensitive issues" would be forbidden—even in Parliament. These issues included the special position of Malays and Borneo's ethnic groups and the power of the Malay sultans. Bahasa Malaysia was made the country's official language. It would be used for all government business.

Most non-Malays disliked the amended constitution. Just as unpopular was 1971's New Economic Policy. This 20-year plan hoped to achieve a better balance of wealth by offering Malays special privileges in business, education and government. Many Indian and Chinese citizens felt discriminated against. After all, many of them had family ties in Malaysia going back over a century.

Years later, then-Prime Minister Mahathir Mohamad explained that Malays needed the policy because "They were very behind the other races in the early days of independence, owning only two percent of

People in Malaysia blend the modern and the traditional, like this Muslim woman with her cellphone.

the economic wealth of the country and had very few educated at the university level. Their participation in business was minimal."[1]

In 1973, the National Front (in Malay, Barisan Nasional) was born. A multiracial political party combining 13 different groups—including Malays, Chinese, Indians, and Muslims—it was an important step in convincing non-Malays that the elected government would represent their interests as well.

Doubts about the plan were reduced by the country's economic success. Although there were other reasons, the New Economic Policy was credited with helping the country achieve steady growth. "As a result of the New Economic Policy," Mohamad said, "[Malays] now have 20 percent of the wealth and many have university qualifications. And besides being in various professions, they own numerous successful businesses."[2] Still, the New Economic Policy was ended in 1991, partly because of its unpopularity.

Appointed by the country's monarch in 1981, Mohamad was the country's longest-serving prime minister. He remained in office for 22 years, overseeing a period of rapid growth during which the standard of living for most Malaysians improved.

The country became a manufacturing center, with over one-third of workers employed building cars, refining oil and processing some of the raw materials like rubber, hardwoods, and petroleum the country has in abundance. By the late 1990s, the country had attracted more high-tech industries as well.

FYI FACT:

Although Malaysia has worked hard to secure a reputation for religious freedom, one faith is excluded. Passport holders from the Jewish state of Israel encounter greater obstacles to visiting than others, there are no Jewish holidays in Malaysia, and anti-Semitic (or anti-Jewish) statements regularly appear in the media.

Malaysia is a tiger, an Asian country with a high growth rate. Like Singapore, Taiwan, and South Korea, it has enjoyed growth that is often significantly higher than more developed countries like the United States.

Unfortunately, the late 1990s and late 2000s saw a pair of financial crises that slowed the country's growth. By the time Mohamad stepped down in 2003, the country was back on track. Deputy Prime Minister Abdullah Ahmad Badawi succeeded him, presiding over another period of growth and achievement.

To maintain this momentum, Malaysia has embarked on an ambitious program. Called Vision 2020, the plan is to be a fully developed nation by 2020. To reach this goal, the country must continue its high growth and employment. Malaysia must continue to generate money from traditional industries like oil and rubber while developing its high-tech sector.

As an eye doctor, former Prime Minister Mohamad knows that 2020 means excellent vision. To him, "2020 for Malaysia implies this clear vision of where we want to go and where we want to be."[3] By having a clear vision of the future while not forgetting the past, Malaysia has made itself a significant power in the present.

This worker is employed by Royal Selangor, the world's largest pewter manufacturer.

A cobbler's son, Jimmy Choo used his talents to build a billion-dollar designer shoe company.

Chapter 9

Malaysians Who Have Made Their Mark

Many people have made significant contributions to Malaysian prosperity and to enhancing its image around the world. Here are just a few.

Jimmy Choo (1961–): Choo was born into a family of shoemakers in Penang. His father wanted him to continue in the family business. "When I first started, my father wouldn't let me make a shoe," Choo remembered in later life. "Instead, he said: 'Sit and watch, sit and watch.' For months and months I did that."[1] Finally, at the age of 11, Choo was allowed to produce his first pair of shoes. To pursue his craft, the young man traveled to England and enrolled at Cordwainers Technical College. He graduated with honors in 1983. Three years later, he opened his first shop in a former hospital building. In 1988, he hit the big time: *Vogue* magazine featured his shoes in an eight-page spread. Since then, he has become one of the most famous shoemakers in the world. Princess Diana became a client, and wore Jimmy Choos everywhere she went. Today, his shoes cost hundreds and even thousands of dollars a pair.

Nicol David (1983–): Like many young people all over the world, Nicol David began playing sports in her home town of Penang when she was just 5 years old. In her case, the sport was squash. Unlike almost every other young person, however, she became a world champion—seven times. She has also been a gold medalist at the

51

One of the world's best squash players, Nicol David is working to make the game an Olympic sport.

Commonwealth Games, the British Open, and the Asian Games. She was the first Asian woman to be ranked number 1 in international women's squash. In fact, many people believe that she is the greatest female squash player of all time. She is actively engaged in the campaign to make squash into an Olympic sport. If she is successful, there's a good chance she could add even more gold to her already impressive collection.

Yusof Ghani (1950–): Ghani began his professional career as a graphic designer. He transitioned to fine arts when he received a scholarship to attend school in the United States. Several years later, he hailed a cab after visiting New York City's famed Metropolitan Museum of Art. The driver asked Ghani a life-changing question. As he later explained, "He was a Nigerian and he questioned me about the role of art. He told me that in Africa, you get people starving but yet here in New York, people are paying millions for paintings. What can the paintings do? After a state of confusion, I found an answer. Why don't I use art as a medium of communication? I can use art to tell the world how I feel."[2] Ghani began exploring the ways in which paintings could convey messages about life's obstacles. His Protest series opposed U.S. involvement in Nicaragua and El Salvador and was very well received at its first showing in Washington, D.C. Since then, his work has emphasized a variety of themes. He also teaches art in Malaysia and sculpts and writes in addition to his painting.

Dr. Sheikh Muszaphar Shukor (1972–): Shukor was trained as an orthopedic surgeon. In 2007 he was selected to become Malaysia's first astronaut. He blasted off on October 10th and spent nine days at the International Space Station, where he conducted numerous experiments. When he returned, he became a regular participant in space research programs and spoke frequently to groups of young people, encouraging them to follow their dreams. In 2010 he was named an ambassador of Malaysia's national reading program, which helps schoolchildren to improve their reading skills. Because of his accomplishments, he has been named one of the world's 500 most influential Muslims. And somehow he finds time in his busy schedule to do occasional modeling!

Michelle Yeoh (1962–): Born in the mining town of Ipoh in West Malaysia, Yeoh originally wanted to become a professional dancer. But an injury ended that ambition. Instead, she went on to become the most famous Malaysian film actress, with a specialty in action movies. Her first major role was in the 1992 Jackie Chan movie *Police Story 3: Super Cop*. Five years later she co-starred with Pierce Brosnan in the

Besides being an astronaut and an orthopedic surgeon, Dr. Sheikh Muszaphar Shukor (on the left) also works as a model. He's seen here with other space explorers bound for the International Space Station in 2007.

James Bond film *Tomorrow Never Dies*. In 2008 she was featured in *The Mummy: Tomb of the Dragon Emperor*. She is especially known for doing her own stunts, a risky practice that can result in serious injuries. She has received many honors for her work. In 1997, *People* magazine named her one of the 50 Most Beautiful People in the World. Three years later, the British Academy of Film and Television Arts nominated her for best actress for her work in *Crouching Tiger, Hidden Dragon*. In 2008, the movie-rating website Rotten Tomatoes called her the best action heroine of all time. And *People* listed her as one of the 35 All-Time Screen Beauties in 2009. She was the only Asian actress to be included.

Michelle Yeoh's acting in big-budget films has helped make her a household name across the globe.

Malaysian

Mango Chicken

Indians and Chinese who moved to Malaysia brought their own recipes. Many traditional meals have been changed by adding Malay ingredients. This native dish relies on mangos. An easy-to-find fruit in Malaysia, it can be found in-season in most grocery stores.

   The recipe includes a marinade—a sauce in which meat is soaked—along with a separate sauce. There is quite a bit of chopping and slicing. You will want an adult to help.

Ingredients:
½ small red bell pepper cut into chunks
½ small green bell pepper cut into chunks
½ onion cut in quarters
½ medium ripe green mango peeled, pitted, and slivered
8 ounces skinless, boneless chicken cut into bite-size pieces
2 tablespoons oil

Optional:
2 tablespoons chili powder (spicy)
1 tablespoon oyster sauce (fishy)

Marinade: Combine 1 teaspoon cornstarch, ½ teaspoon salt, ½ teaspoon sugar, and a pinch of black pepper.

Sauce: Blend 2 tablespoons ketchup, one tablespoon Worcestershire sauce, and one tablespoon steak sauce. Add one teaspoon of honey, 2 tablespoons juice (mango or pineapple), pinch of sugar and salt, and one teaspoon apple cider vinegar, balsamic or black vinegar.

Instructions:
1. Marinate the chicken for 10 minutes.
2. Heat oil in a wok or covered pan. Add the peppers and onions, cooking them until slightly charred. Set aside.
3. Heat more oil and add the marinated chicken pieces and mango slivers. Stir and cover wok or pan. Cook on medium high heat for two minutes.
4. Remove cover, add sauce and stir until boiling. Cover, lower heat and let simmer until chicken is completely cooked. If a sample piece is pink or watery in the middle, toss it back in and keep cooking.
5. Add the onions and peppers.
6. Stir and dish up over rice. Enjoy!

Malaysian Kite

In Malaysia adults enjoy hobbies that might seem childish—like flying kites and spinning tops. Then again, kites are for everyone!

Materials
- One 10" x 12" square of tissue paper or light silk for the sail
- One piece of balsa wood for the kite's spine, 9" x ³⁄₁₆" x ¹⁄₁₆"
- One 11" x ³⁄₁₆" x ¹⁄₁₆" piece of balsa wood for the top spar (part of the frame)
- Two 6" x ³⁄₁₆" x ¹⁄₁₆" pieces of balsa wood for the tail spreaders
- Kite line 24" crochet or buttonhole thread
- 12" piece of kite line
- Heavy paper or cardboard for the pattern
- Glue
- Blunt needle
- Balloon straw or wooden dowel

Instructions
1. Draw a grid of one-inch squares on heavy paper or cardboard. Draw half of the sail and cut it out.
2. Mark where the frame should be, then fold the tissue paper in half and trace the pattern onto the sail. Cut out both sides of the kite together.
3. Apply glue along the spine, attaching it to the sail. Glue the spars and attach them as well, using the pattern beneath the sail to help. Glue paper patches over the ends of the spine and spars.
4. Using a blunt needle, thread the kite line through the sail at the bridle. Tie the end of the kite line around the spine and spar.
5. Tie a bowline to the ends of the tail spreaders and glue the tails to the sail. Fly the kite on two feet of kite line attached to a balloon straw or wooden dowel.

Dates BCE

3000	The Orang Asli migrate to the Malay Peninsula from China and Tibet.
1000	The first Malays settle in Malaysia.
100	Traders from China and India arrive; Indian traders introduce Hindu and Buddhist beliefs and customs.

Dates CE

ca. 100	Kingdom of Langkasuka on the Malay Peninsula begins to flourish.
ca. 1150	Religion of Islam arrives on the Malay Peninsula.
ca. 1400	Sumatran Prince Parameswara flees to Malacca and makes it into a successful trading port.
1414	Mahkota Iskander Shah's conversion to Islam accelerates the spread of the religion.
1511	Portuguese conquer Malacca.
1641	The Dutch drive the Portuguese out of Malacca.
1826	Malacca, Penang, and Singapore form the Straits Settlements colony.
1857	Chinese tin miners found Kuala Lumpur.
1895	Four states combine to form the Federated Malay States.
1942	Japanese troops occupy Malaya.
1948	The Federation of Malaya is formed through the unification of British-ruled territories.
1948	A communist insurgency begins 12 years of unrest.
1957	The Federation of Malaya becomes independent from Britain; Tunka Adbul Rahman becomes prime minister.
1963	Sabah, Sarawak, and Singapore join the Federation of Malaya and form the Federation of Malaysia.
1965	Singapore withdraws from Malaysia to become independent.
1969	Anti-Chinese riots in Kuala Lumpur result in hundreds of deaths.
1970	Tun Abdul Razak becomes prime minister and forms National Front (BN) coalition.
1971	Government of Malaysia introduces minimum quotas for Malays in business and education.
1981	Mahathir Mohamad becomes prime minister.
1990	Sarawak communist insurgents sign peace accord with the government.
1997	An Asian financial crisis depresses economic growth in Malaysia.
2001	Many people are arrested when Malays and Indians clash.
2002	Laws against illegal immigrants go into effect.
2003	Mahathir Mohamad steps down as prime minister; Abdullah Ahmad Badawi replaces him.
2004	A tsumani that devastates parts of Indonesia kills dozens of Malaysians.
2005	Malaysia and Singapore settle a dispute over land reclamation.

2007	A series of floods results in the evacuation of more than 70,000 people.
2008	Prime Minister Badawi's BN coalition maintains power but has lowest percentage of votes in Malaysian history.
2009	Malaysia bans the hiring of foreign workers to protect its citizens from being unemployed.
2011	In Kuala Lumpur, police use tear gas to break up a rally for electoral reform.
2012	Three thousand environmental activists protest building a refinery in Pahang state.
2014	Malaysia launches ambitious tourism campaign to bring millions of tourists and their money to visit.

CHAPTER NOTES

Chapter Two: Malaysian History
1. Simon Richmond, *Malaysia, Singapore & Brunei* (Footscray, Australia: The Lonely Planet, 2009), p. 30.

Chapter Four: Celebrate
1. "Constitution of Malaysia," Constitution Finder. T.C. Williams School of Law, University of Richmond, Richmond, Virginia. http://confinder.richmond.edu/admin/docs/malaysia.pdf
2. "Diwali," BBC—Religions: Diwali. http://www.bbc.co.uk/religion/religions/hinduism/holydays/diwali.shtml

Chapter Five: Europeans Arrive
1. Tomé Pires and Armando Cortesão. *The Suma Oriental of Tomé Pires: An Account of the East, from the Red Sea to Japan, Written in Malacca and India in 1512-1515.* (Surrey, United Kingdom: Ashgate, 2010), p. lxxv.
2. Ibid., p. 2.

Chapter Six: Rise of Cities, Rise of Malaysia
1. "The Petronas Towers," *The Skyscraper Museum.* http://www.skyscraper.org/TALLEST_TOWERS/t_petronas.htm
2. Panjab Mishra, *From the Ruins of Empire: the Intellectuals Who Remade Asia* (New York: Farrar, Straus and Giroux, 2012), p. 246.

Chapter Seven: A New Malaysia
1. Panjab Mishra, *From the Ruins of Empire: the Intellectuals Who Remade Asia* (New York: Farrar, Straus and Giroux, 2012), p. 251.

Chapter Eight: 20-20 Vision
1. Mahathir Mohamad, "Malaysia on Track for 2020 Vision." http://freedownloadb.com/pdf/malaysia-on-track-for-2020-vision-welcome-to-the-united-5643155.html
2. Ibid.

Chapter Nine: Malaysians Who Have Made Their Mark
1. "Jimmy Choo: Biography." Biography.com. http://www.biography.com/people/jimmy-choo-20692491
2. "Interview with Yusof," Yusof Ghani—Malaysian Abstract Artist. http://www.yusofghani.com/interview.htm

FURTHER READING / WORKS CONSULTED

FURTHER READING

Books

Di Piazza, Francesca. *Malaysia in Pictures.* Minneapolis: Twenty First Century Books, 2006.

Heinrichs, Ann. *Malaysia.* New York: Children's Press, 2004.

Hosking, Wayne. *Asian Kites.* Boston, Massachusetts: Tuttle Publishing, 2005.

McNair, Sylvia. *Malaysia.* New York: Childrens Press, 2002.

Munan, Heidi, and Yuk Yee Foo. *Malaysia (Cultures of the World).* 3rd ed. New York: Benchmark Books, 2012.

On the Internet

Public Holidays: Malaysia
    http://publicholidays.com.my/

National Geographic: Orangutan
    http://animals.nationalgeographic.com/animals/mammals/orangutan/?source=A-to-Z

National Geographic: Sumatran Rhinoceros
    http://animals.nationalgeographic.com/animals/mammals/sumatran-rhinoceros/

National Geographic: Malaysia Guide:
    http://travel.nationalgeographic.com/travel/countries/malaysia-guide/

The Sarawak Museum
    http://www.museum.sarawak.gov.my/index.php

WORKS CONSULTED

Books

Belliveau, Denis and Francis Donnell. *In the Footsteps of Marco Polo.* Lanham, Maryland: Rowman & Littlefield, 2008.

de Ledesma, Charles. *The Rough Guide to Malaysia, Singapore and Brunei.* 5th ed. New York: Rough Guides, 2006.

Eveland, Jennifer. *Frommer's Singapore & Malaysia.* 7th ed. Hoboken, New Jersey: Wiley, 2011.

Heidhues, Mary F. *Southeast Asia: A Concise History.* New York: Thames & Hudson, 2000.

Mishra, Pankaj. *From the Ruins of Empire: the Intellectuals Who Remade Asia.* New York: Farrar, Straus and Giroux, 2012.

Richmond, Simon. *Malaysia, Singapore & Brunei.* Footscray, Australia: The Lonely Planet, 2009.

Tarling, N. *The Cambridge History of Southeast Asia.* Cambridge, United Kingdom: Cambridge University Press, 2008.

Wallace, Alfred Russel. *The Malay Archipelago, the land of the orang-utan and the bird of paradise*. London: Macmillan, 1869. Project Gutenberg E-Book edition: The Malay Archipelago: Volume I, 2008, Rev. 2011 http://www.gutenberg.org/files/2530/2530-h/2530-h.htm#2HCH0001

Williams, China. *Southeast Asia on a Shoestring*. 15th ed. Footscray, Australia: Lonely Planet, 2010.

DVD

Thailand, Malaysia & Laos. Dir. Justine Shapiro. Perf. N/A. Escapi New Media Studios, 2004.

On the Internet

BBC News: Malaysia Profile
  http://www.bbc.co.uk/news/world-asia-pacific-15356257

BBC News: Malaysia Profile—Timeline
  http://www.bbc.co.uk/news/world-asia-pacific-15391762

Five Pillars of Islam
  http://www.saudiembassy.net/about/country-information/Islam/five_pillars_of_Islam.aspx

Wonderful Malaysia: Georgetown
  http://www.wonderfulmalaysia.com/georgetown-city-penang-malaysia.htm

Malaysian Mango Chicken
  http://rasamalaysia.com/malaysian-mango-chicken/2/

Orang Asli
  http://www.malaysiasite.nl/orangeng.htm

Carnivorous Plants
  http://www.petpitcher.com/home

Sepilok Orang Utan Sanctuary
  http://www.sabahtourism.com/sabah-malaysian-borneo/en/destination/32/

The History of Shadow Puppet Shows in Indonesia and Malaysia
  http://www.swiss-belhotel.com/articles/history-shadow-puppet-shows-indonesia-malaysia/

amending (uh-MEHN-ding)—Changing.

arabesques (air-uh-BESKS)—Ornamental designs consisting of intertwined flowing lines.

carnivorous (cahr-NIHV-ohr-uss)—Eating meat.

causeway (CAWZ-way)—A roadway that travels over water.

colony (CAHL-uh-nee)—A region controlled by another country, which often exploits its resources.

deposed (dee-POZED)—Removed from power.

flotilla (floh-TIHL-uh)—A fleet of ships or boats.

halal (huh-LAWL)—Food which is specially prepared according to Islamic law.

insurgency (in-SIHR-juhn-see)—A rebellion, usually armed, against a government.

sanctioned (SANK-shunned)—Allowed, legally permitted.

shophouses (SHAHP-hou-zehz)—Stores that open onto a sidewalk or street and also serve as the residence of their owners.

verandahs (vihr-ANN-duhz)—Roofed platforms that may be partially enclosed, extending along the side of a building

wizened (WIH-zund)—Shriveled or wrinkled with age.

INDEX

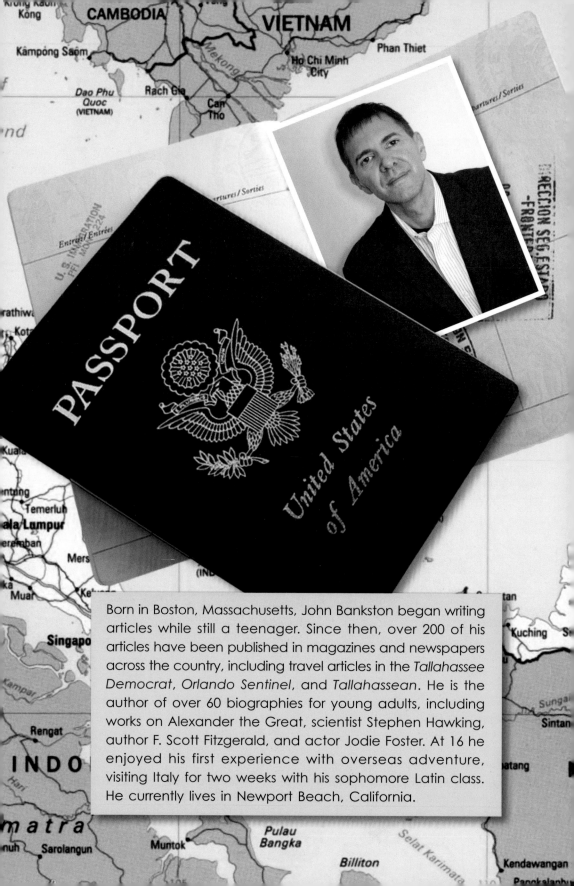

Born in Boston, Massachusetts, John Bankston began writing articles while still a teenager. Since then, over 200 of his articles have been published in magazines and newspapers across the country, including travel articles in the *Tallahassee Democrat*, *Orlando Sentinel*, and *Tallahassean*. He is the author of over 60 biographies for young adults, including works on Alexander the Great, scientist Stephen Hawking, author F. Scott Fitzgerald, and actor Jodie Foster. At 16 he enjoyed his first experience with overseas adventure, visiting Italy for two weeks with his sophomore Latin class. He currently lives in Newport Beach, California.